THE LAST TIME I SAW YOU

poems by

Diane Elayne Dees

Finishing Line Press
Georgetown, Kentucky

THE LAST TIME
I SAW YOU

Copyright © 2022 by Diane Elayne Dees
ISBN 978-1-64662-990-9 First Edition
All rights reserved under International and Pan-American Copyright Conventions. No part of this book may be reproduced in any manner whatsoever without written permission from the publisher, except in the case of brief quotations embodied in critical articles and reviews.

ACKNOWLEDGMENTS

The author is grateful to Todd Spiker for his help with this chapbook.

Publisher: Leah Huete de Maines
Editor: Christen Kincaid
Cover Art and Design: Diana Souza, linkedin.com/in/dianasouza
Author Photo: Diane Elayne Dees

Order online: www.finishinglinepress.com
also available on amazon.com

Author inquiries and mail orders:
Finishing Line Press
PO Box 1626
Georgetown, Kentucky 40324
USA

Table of Contents

Everything Was Fine 1
Memorial 2
What It's Like 3
Birthday 4
A Dream 5
Distance 6
Your Careers 7
After Katrina 8
You Changed 9
The Emails I Didn't Save 10
Images of You 11
Forgotten Lives 12
Cats Know 13
Ritual 14
Your Crooked House... 15
Things You Gave Me 16
Something I Gave You 17
Attachment 18
Philosophical 19
The Accident 20
Transcendence 21
Shamanism 22
An Offering 23
Things I Cannot Know.. 24
Your Last Review 25
The Last Time I Saw You 26
A Limited Depth of Field 27
Comfort 28
Float 29
New Routines 30
Ghosts 31

For D. Eric

Everything Was Fine

Six days before your birthday,
I learned that you were dead.
We were somewhat estranged,
yet it seemed odd that I didn't hear
from you at Christmas.
I didn't hear from you, it turns out,
because you left us in November.
The doctors who misdiagnosed you
said your life could be cut short,
but you took matters into your own hands,
just like you did decades ago,
when you cured yourself
of the arthritis that crippled you
and confined you to your bed.
You told me you were symptom-free,
and I stopped worrying about you.
But then I sent you an email—
and you never replied.
I was going to make you a birthday card
because I was tired of our distance.
I would have sent you loving greetings,
And I would have told you—
in my own way— that between us,
everything was fine.

Memorial

Your memorial celebration was held
in early March in New Orleans.
I didn't know about it; I didn't know
that you had died. Had I known,
I would have gone, unknowingly
immersing myself in the virus that grew
faster in the City That Care Forgot
than anywhere else in the world.
You would have wanted to spare me that,
and I feel grateful to have not been in that room.
But I also feel sad that I missed my chance
to stand up and say what I know to be true—
that your life transcended viruses and disease
and prejudice—that it also transcended ignorance
and careless doctors and failed organs.
I am saying it now.

What It's Like

I used to wonder what it would be like
to have a dear friend die.
Would I feel numb? Would I linger
in disbelief? Would I feel regret?
Or would I simply fall apart?
I think that it is all of these things.
We hadn't seen each other in a few years,
though we were always in touch.
I know that if you were here,
you would find some backdoor
way to suggest that I feel gratitude.
And I do, but right now,
numb is at the head of the line.
I am no stranger to grief,
but this is a new version,
and I need time—while I stumble
over regrets, memories, lost years,
unfinished conversations,
and all the other odds and ends
I've stuffed into the dark corners
of my overcrowded consciousness—
time to clear a path,
time to find peace.

Birthday

Today is your birthday.
I always make you a card,
but now, all I can do
is make you a poem.
I honor everything you loved:
art of every period and genre,
cats of every stripe and patch,
the drums of Buddhism,
the streets of New Orleans,
your cameras,
the color purple,
your friends,
the present moment.

A Dream

So many years ago, I dreamed
that you had died. I was lost, drifting
down Canal Street, when you appeared
in front of a parking meter,
in your worn-out jeans and signature
purple plaid shirt, and you said,
"I've come to tell you that it's okay."
You disappeared—and then I woke up.
But I never forgot that dream,
and now, I need to remember
every color, every detail, of its fabric.

Distance

After I moved across the lake,
we rarely saw each other.
You were often busy,
or I wanted to make a quick trip
to the city and get back home.
You said, for years,
that you would visit me,
but I knew you wouldn't.
It troubled me that we saw so little of one another;
sometimes, I thought, "what if one of us dies?"—
and then one of us did.
I am a woman burdened with regrets.
Another one would crush me,
so I accept that our volumes of emails
kept us securely bound in our lifelong friendship.
All the same, sometimes I missed
the familiar comfort of your languid vowels,
the ease of your cat-like gait,
the fusion of cultures that was your face.

Your Careers

You were the only art critic
I'd ever known. I confess
to not always reading your reviews
because—like everyone else—
I was busy doing other things,
and because reading them
made me want to visit exhibitions
in New Orleans, and the city
seemed farther and farther away
as the years went by.
You were many things—
curator, editor, archivist,
artist—and now I look
at your book of photographs,
bask in your unique sensibility,
and admire your photographer's eye.
But mostly, I feel honored
that you were my friend.

After Katrina

After the floods, you stayed with us
for a few days. You couldn't get home,
and to make matters worse,
your beloved cat had been killed
right before the levees broke.
It was the only time I had ever seen you sad.
Each day, our sister cats sat, side by side,
outside the guest bathroom, and waited
patiently for you to come out of the shower
and join us in the living room.
It was an amusing sight, but I knew
that it was also a gift—
a gift that only those cats
would have known to give you.

You Changed

I met you for lunch after not seeing you
for a long time, and I had to hide my shock.
You, who had always appeared ageless,
suddenly looked old. You hardly ate anything,
and you told me that you had lost interest
in food, music, and almost everything else.
You said you believed you had meditated
so much, you had lost almost all desires.
But I wondered if Katrina had drained you
of the capacity to hunger for things
you used to take for granted.
None of us escaped without scars,
none of us will ever be quite the same.

The Emails I Didn't Save

I wish I had saved your emails,
not for sentimental reasons,
but because they were filled
with things I learned from you
about art, history, religion, and culture,
about philosophy, architecture and music.
I thought I knew a lot, but then
I would hear from you,
and I would realize
how much I didn't know.
I wondered how you knew so much,
and how you remembered it all.
Sometimes I felt ignorant
in your virtual presence,
which was both humbling and annoying;
I understand now what a gift that was.

Images of You

I have only a few photographs of you,
but they neatly span the decades
of our friendship. From the dark drama
of your thick brown hair
and neatly trimmed beard
to the silver and white
of your final decade,
they are all portraits of a man
who may be serious,
but who may also be amused—
it was always hard to tell with you.
In my favorite, you are in your fifties:
Your black and gray striped shirt
perfectly matches your black hair
streaked with gray,
and your already-silver mustache.
Writing about your own ethereal photographs,
you said that we are all merely the dreams
of the universe. Your images make you real
to me, and so you are—though perhaps
we are also dreams, you and I,
and our eternal story evolves
even as I write this.

Forgotten Lives

You fed all the neighborhood strays
and feral cats. When they were injured,
you took them to the doctor,
paid their medical expenses,
took care of them as best you could.
When they died, you dug their graves,
buried them, and spoke words
that honored their forgotten lives.
When my beloved patch tortoiseshell died,
I contacted you because you knew her
and had shared our space with her
and her mischievous tabby sister.
How was I to know, when I sent the message,
that you had just put down your shovel?
Sadness over cats is like joy over cats:
it courses into the very depths of our beings.
You always made room for both.

Cats Know

What will they do now, the cats
who roamed your neighborhood,
and counted on you for food, water,
medicine, and—at the end—
a proper burial? Will someone step in
and care for them, or will they wander
from street to street,
their bones almost exposed,
and their fates left to whoever
put the poison out?
Cats know many things;
I suspect they know that you died.
I hope they also know
how to find a new lifeline
in the streets of New Orleans,
which few tread as lightly as you.

Ritual

In the golden age of New Orleans,
when ritual defined everything we did,
Sunday mornings belonged to us.
We spent hours at the restaurant
where the streetcars turned around,
and sometimes braved the line at the Bluebird.
I don't remember when we stopped sharing
plates of pancakes and omeletes,
or *why* we stopped. Everything changes,
but when rituals cease, something is stolen
that cannot be replaced. I can still see you
seated at a wobbly cafe table,
alternating bites of toast with profound opinions
and deliciously wicked observations.
The heavenly smell of coffee surrounds us,
a Sunday morning incense lifting the prayers
of the faithful above the levee,
along the Street of Dreams,
and into the haze of our futures.

Your Crooked House

You lived near a levee
that cut the streets off
at an angle, and your house
was built on that angle,
like a distorted playing piece
on an abandoned Monopoly board.
I imagine that it summoned you
like a metaphysical magnet
searching for a resident
who could not abide straight lines
or live in a box.
When your landlord died,
you upended his wreck of a house
like you were Indiana Jones,
unearthing everything from 30-year-old
magazines to long forgotten sandwiches.
Days later, you found his hand-written will,
and the crooked house was legally yours,
as the Universe undoubtedly intended,
and as the house itself—
in its old age—desired.

Things You Gave Me

A collection of Monet's cooking journals,
for my wedding.
A copy of a slyly brilliant photo
your father took seventy-five years ago
for the old New Orleans Camera Club.
Numerous books,
from your French Market bookseller days.
My astrological chart,
which you carefully drew
for me, and which I cannot find.
A signed copy of your most notable book.
Photos you took of me when we were young:
I'm in black velvet and rhinestones
and riding in a subversive Mardi Gras parade;
I'm in a booth at lunch with a movie star's daughter.
Forty years of memorabilia doesn't help me
sort out anything about you or me.
But they are things that I can touch and look at,
fragments that keep you in this dimension,
artifacts that ease the pain of your absence.

Something I Gave You

I was happy to introduce you to Tolle,
but surprised that you hadn't read
his books. You bought the first one,
and were so taken with it,
you immediately read it again.
For years, you said, you had searched
for such a synthesis of everything
you believed. I was not accustomed
to hearing this much enthusiasm
from you about *anything*.
I was proud to have made it possible,
and suggested you read the second book.
You said you planned to,
but I don't know if you ever did—
and that's just one more conversation
that we will never have, though,
as I'm sure you would tell me,
what we did and did not do
has nothing to do with the Now.

Attachment

Someone broke your heart.
I didn't know you had a girlfriend
until you told me she had left you.
You were thoughtful and stoic about it,
but I kept trying to comfort you
because you must have had a reason
for telling me. It can be difficult,
offering comfort to *any* man;
it was a special challenge,
offering comfort to you, a Buddhist.
I understood that you maintained perspective,
that you knew how to separate pain
from suffering, that you were able
to just observe your thoughts.
But I tried to comfort you,
because I also understood
that she broke your heart.

Philosophical

We both liked living alone,
though, unlike you, I married.
When I divorced,
I wanted you to be angry
on my behalf, but you were,
of course, philosophical.

I thought that was the end
of the subject, but it turns out
that—in your later years—
you had considered marriage.
But the woman went away—
and you were philosophical.

Then *you* went away.
And I want to be like you,
but I am on a journey
in which the path is littered
with regret, the view is blocked
by tears, and it's a very long way
to Philosophical.

The Accident

I remember the accident.
You fell off the bike
and your body became
a repository for pain.
You suffered terribly for months,
though I didn't know,
for a very long time,
just how much you suffered.

It wasn't your first experience
with pain, but it was the first
one you couldn't solve
with your gift for blending
vitamins and minerals.
There was no cocktail
that could make your days
bearable, so you opted
for a new treatment—
you opted for acceptance.

This is how you embraced
Buddhism—you kept the pain
and dropped the suffering.
Then your body healed,
and your soul followed.
I always admired you for that,
and now I wonder:
Did I ever tell you?

Transcendence

When your physical pain
was at its most excruciating,
when you didn't know
how you could bear it,
you sought anything
for which you could be grateful.
You became preoccupied
with gratitude instead of pain,
and gratitude became your medicine.

You did not tell me this
until many years had passed,
and hearing it stunned me.
To read about the power of gratitude
is one thing; to know someone
who applied it as a balm
to mitigate the fire of pain
is a revelation.

Gratitude and pain
are both perceptions;
your photographer's eye
was illuminated by a light
deep within you, a light
that guided you to see
not just shapes and shadows,
but also, the self who lives
on the other side of pain.

Shamanism

I went to see a shaman,
and when I told you,
you were all over it,
teaching me about shamanism,
unfolding its history, explaining
what different kinds of shamans do
and where and how they do it.
I learned so much from you,
but I never learned
why my soul retrieval failed,
and why, after a painful extraction,
the grief, fear and limiting words
are still stuck somewhere inside me.
This was something I needed to discuss
with you, but we never got around to it.
Now I keep my channels open,
for it would be just like you
to bump into my spirit animal
and send it flying back to me
with the answers I seek.

An Offering

I was angry with you.
You dared me to convince you
that writing all those poems about my grief
and regret could possibly help me,
but you wouldn't listen when I tried to explain
to you that it did. You told me to go ahead
and enjoy my misery. You struck me repeatedly
with a bludgeon of Buddhism,
refusing to understand
the value of a poet's catharsis.
You lectured me on the toxicity of my thinking,
and I understood what you were saying,
but I was grieving the best I knew how,
by translating my fear and sadness into words.
Words are all I have; poetry is sacred.
I pulled back my trust,
I stopped sending you my poems.
Now I am grieving your death
and writing poems about my grief,
unintentionally creating a koan for you,
and awaiting your answer.

Things I Cannot Know

I introduced you, quite innocently,
to one of my dearest friends,
and she made your life miserable.
Eventually, she moved away,
but not without first picking a fight
with me. She and I never spoke again,
but you and I talked about her for years.
The betrayal was different for each of us,
but the sting was sharp and long-lasting.
Then, one day, the subject was dropped,
the chapter was finished. But now I wonder:
Did she talk about you for years?
Did she wish that things had gone differently?
Does she know that you are gone?

Your Last Review

I just read your last review,
published two days after you died.
You reviewed the work
of one of your best friends,
a photographer I greatly admire.
You described the exhibition as a mix
of "dreams, art history and poetry,"
and you discussed the overlap
of cultural history and the psyche.
That was always one of our favorite subjects,
the Jungian lodestone that pulls us
through life as the moon pulls the tides.
But—just as more is going on
in the photographer's surrealistic photos
than a quick glance would imply—
perhaps more is going on in your words.
That this is your final comment
on the nature of art and life—
a meditation on the transcendent art
of someone so dear to you—
feels eerily complete in a way
that makes me shiver,
but also makes me smile.

The Last Time I Saw You

The last time I saw you,
it was at the house you inherited
from your brother—the house
where you ran your arts organization.
You were uncharacteristically animated
as you walked me through the collection.
Much of the art told stories about your family,
a complex, fascinating history centered in Belize,
featuring characters of storybook proportion.
You explained to me what had led you to Buddhism,
and I knew you were really telling me
how to resolve my own grief and trauma.
Your Siamese cat charmingly interrupted
our tea time. We stood on your balcony,
with a view of the famous indie singer's house,
then took a brief walk down the block,
with its banana trees and crayon-colored houses.
I resolved—the next time I visited—
it would be in the house where you lived,
the house I hadn't seen in decades.
But there would be no coffee-fueled lost afternoon,
no neighborhood stroll down memory lane—
because that was the last time I saw you.

A Limited Depth of Field

My long-term memory is a collage
of shadows and dimly visible colored lights.
Atmosphere and emotion occupy
most of the space, but there is clarity
in random details.

We are sitting in your living room
in the house near the levee,
listening to saxophone music
oozing out of your ancient German speakers.
It is the cleanest, most resonant sound
I have ever heard.

We are at a dinner party
at the Columns Hotel,
and a rare New Orleans ice storm hits.
A few brave souls drive home,
but the rest of us rent a room,
stay up all night, and order endless drinks
from a woman we insist on calling Babette.

We are in the office of the weekly newspaper,
exchanging gossip, or at Tipitina's,
chatting with James Booker,
or we are at an art show
where all of the artists are our friends.

I long to remember more details,
but must be content with savoring
the ones I recall, and with knowing
that so many of my days were richer
because you were there.

Comfort

I wish I had one of your shirts.
I could wrap it around my body
while I drink whiskey
and listen to James Booker albums.
I would probably cry,
but I would be okay
because my shirt would be lined
with you.

Float

My divorce ripped me apart, and I realized
that my marriage had all but destroyed me.
You knew nothing about the biology
of trauma, but you understood its essence.
"Float," you told me, "as though on a balmy sea."
And I tried, but everything in me felt too heavy.
Then a yoga instructor told me to float my body
toward the sky, and I thought of you.
And when the host of a writing workshop
told us to float, then to write about floating,
I thought of you.
I'm still learning to float, still searching
for a balmy sea. I think of you,
and I wonder:
What is it like for you now,
to float?

New Routines

Confined to my house while we all wait
for the pandemic to fade away,
I adjust to a new routine. I do more yoga,
take virtual classes, wipe down my doorknobs.
And I return again and again to the headline,
"art critic dies." I know what the words mean,
but I have to be sure that I really saw them
and didn't dream them or imagine them
or hallucinate them while I was in lockdown haze.
Your photo is published, so it must be real;
I tell myself this every day. The time will come
when we are all released from these new routines,
but I wonder when I will be released
from reading "art critic dies" over and over,
hoping that the words will convince me
that you are really gone.

Ghosts

I saw a startling photograph
of dozens of ghostly, glowing female figures
extended from floor to ceiling in a museum
in Buenos Aires. It looked like a picture
you might have taken, of an exhibition
you would have longed to review.
The artist described his work
as both calming and agitating,
moving and fearful,
representing the insignificance
of our consciousness,
and our oneness with nature.
I was mesmerized by the photo,
and longed to see the exhibition.
And in that faintest of moments
when the veil between our two worlds
seemed as fragile and luminous as the skirts
on the women in the photo—
I copied the link to the page,
as if to send it to you.
Such a moment, so brief, cannot be measured.
It is time not calculated by clocks,
but by the glowing presence of our souls,
both moving and fearful.

Diane Elayne Dees lives in Covington, Louisiana, just across Lake Pontchartrain from New Orleans. A retired psychotherapist, Diane has also worked as a public relations specialist, and as a speech communication instructor at Tulane University. Her poetry, short fiction and creative nonfiction have been published in numerous journals and anthologies, and her poetry has also been read on several radio shows, including Martha Stewart Living Radio.

Diane is the author of the chapbook, *Coronary Truth* (Kelsay Books), and the forthcoming chapbook, *The Wild Parrots of Marigny* (Querencia Press); she is also the author of three Origami Poems Project microchaps. Diane publishes *Women Who Serve*, a blog that delivers news and commentary on women's professional tennis throughout the world. Her author blog is *Diane Elayne Dees: Poet and Writer-at-Large*.

www.ingramcontent.com/pod-product-compliance
Lightning Source LLC
LaVergne TN
LVHW041604070426
835507LV00011B/1302